Can You Do This?

Diana Noonan

Contents

Do You Get Bored?

What do you do when you get bored?
You could try these fun things to pass
the time.

The Flamingo

1. Stand on one foot.
2. Close your eyes.
3. Now – count to 10.

Did you start to fall over?
That's because your eyes
help you **balance**.

Your Brain

Your **brain** makes you think and move. It uses what your eyes see to help you balance.

The things in this book may seem hard at first. It takes time for your brain to learn new ways to move and think.

The Brain

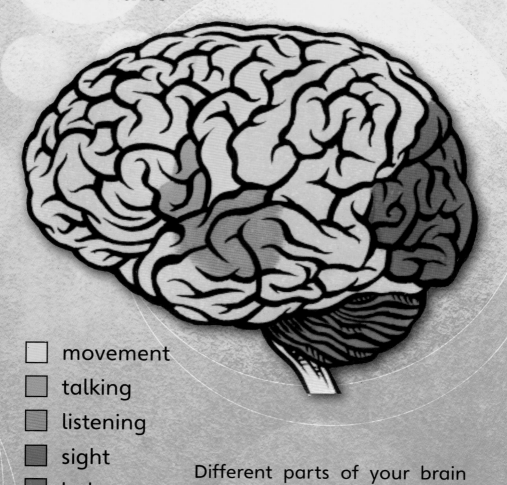

☐ movement
☐ talking
☐ listening
☐ sight
☐ balance

Different parts of your brain help you do different things.

The Monkey

1. Touch your left ear with your right hand like this.
2. Hold your nose with your left hand.

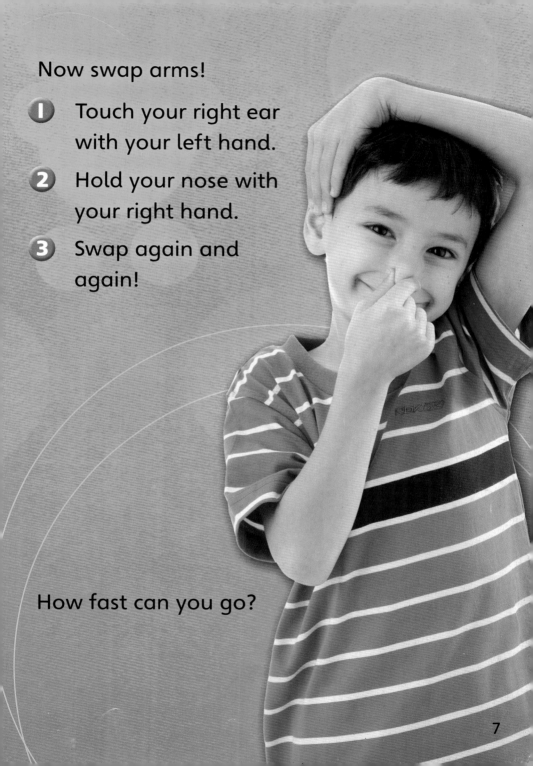

Now swap arms!

1. Touch your right ear with your left hand.

2. Hold your nose with your right hand.

3. Swap again and again!

How fast can you go?

Pat and Rub

1 Pat one hand up and down on top of your head.

2 Rub your other hand round and round on your tummy.

3 Now, try and do both at the same time.

It's hard, isn't it?
Keep trying!

Finger-and-foot challenge

1 Move one foot clockwise round and round in a circle.

2 Now, stop and write the number six in the air with your finger.

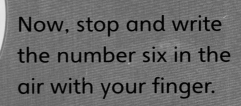

3 Try and do both at
the same time.

It's hard, isn't it?

Keep turning
your foot!

Mirrors

1. Hold up your writing hand.
   Write the letter "D".

2. Now, hold up both hands.

3. Write the letter "D" with both hands at the same time. Write it forwards with your writing hand. Write it backwards with your other hand.

Did you think that was easy? Now try this!

1. Hold up both hands.

2. Write your name forwards with your writing hand. Write it backwards with your other hand.

Tricky Fingers

Get your fingers ready! This seems easy – but is it?

1 Hold out your hand. Keep your fingers together.

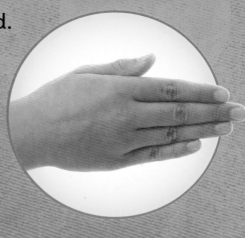

2 Move this finger away from the others.

This one

This one

3 Now, move this finger away from the others.

4 Try to move your fingers apart like this.

It can be hard to move your fingers apart!

People who play the piano are often very good at this **challenge**.

Find Your Fingers

Can you move a finger if a friend points to it and asks you to? What if your arms are crossed?

1 Cross your arms in front of you.

2 Bring your hands together.

3 Lock your fingers together like this.

4 Bring your hands down.

5 Bring them up to your chin.

6 Then, hold them out in front of you.

19

Now, let the fun begin!

7 Ask a friend to point to one of your fingers.

8 Try and wiggle *that* finger.

Your brain has not seen your fingers like this. It will take a while for it to learn which finger is which!

Hole in Your Hand

Warning: This trick may confuse your brain!

1. Roll a piece of paper into a tube.

2 Hold the tube up to one eye, and look through it.

3 Hold the palm of your hand near the end of the tube.

Wow! Your hand looks as if it has a hole in it!

So remember, the next time you are bored, play some tricks on your brain!

Glossary

balance   stay standing without falling over

brain   part of your body that helps you think

challenge   hard task